To

From

Easy Answers to Life's Hard Questions

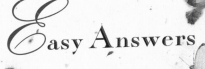

By Lynne Ames

Illustrated and designed by
Kerren Barbas

PETER PAUPER PRESS, INC.
WHITE PLAINS, NEW YORK

Visit us at www.peterpauper.com

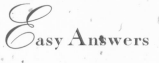

Easy Answers
to Life's
Hard Questions

A friend's secret

is a precious gift;

once entrusted to you,

it must be kept

forever.

Look back

to where

you have been

for a clue to where

you will be going.

*M*arry someone

whose soul you love.

Passion fades,

but friendship remains

forever.

In an argument,

a cool head will soothe a

raging heart most

effectively.

Worry enough to anticipate trouble, but not so much as to bring it about.

Cut your losses quickly

if you make a mistake.

Tell yourself,

"I am human, I can err,"

and then move on.

*T*rue friendship

is a fabric that nothing

can unravel.

Holidays are the

dessert in the meal of

life—

enjoy them

to the last calorie.

Melt the

icy fingers of fear

with the sunshine of hope.

✦

A true friend

never sits in judgment.

Treat your memories
like a movie reel:
rewind and savor
the good scenes;
speed through those that
caused you pain.

The lonely heart
finds love in
unlikely places.

✦

Anger is a flame
that leaves nothing
but ashes.

*L*ove drives us.

Whether for a man or a

woman, a parent or a child,

a place or an ideal, love

energizes virtually all

human activity.

Step by gentle step,

you can overcome the

greatest sorrow.

✦

Every love

is unique.

Pure joy is as rare

and as fleeting

as a wisp of fog.

*B*reak a promise

to a friend, and you've

lost something irreplaceable

within yourself.

Home is that place

where you feel

most safe.

✦

Sometimes, tact

is needed when telling

the truth.

Everyone asks for advice, but few listen.

Marriage is a contract

written in the ink

of passion, respect, and

compromise.

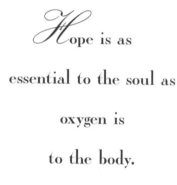

*H*ope is as

essential to the soul as

oxygen is

to the body.

When life becomes

overwhelming, go to a

small quiet corner of

your mind and

remember happier

times.

*E*ven if you can't

forget a hurt, you can

forgive the person

who delivered it.

The sweetest

grapes are picked

from the vineyard of

friendship.

The monster of despair thrives on solitude; your sorrows will shrink as soon as you share them with someone.

Gossip is like a river:

it can always be traced

back to its source.

A jealous friend

is the most dangerous

enemy.

There is no viable
alternative to growing old,
so we might as well do it
with grace and grit.

Generosity is more a matter of mood than money; listen with gentle patience to a friend in need and you bestow a gift greater than gold.

*B*ase your

self-image on one

person's opinion—

your own.

*Y*ou cannot always change circumstances, but you can always change your reaction to them.

*A*n insecure person

will soak up

flattery like a sponge.

If life hands you
a bitter pill, it may
turn out to be the
very medicine that
will make you strong.

A tattered well-read
paperback is worth more
than an unopened
gold-bound volume.

$\mathcal{E}$laborate ritual

is no substitute

for faith.

Having money

allows you to live as

plainly as you choose.

If anything in nature

strikes you as ugly,

you are not appreciating

its diversity.

The flower of
romance grows best in
the soil of good
conversation.

Unfortunately,

virtue may command

admiration but not

always affection.

Guilt is what we feel

when we have

injured others;

shame, when we

have embarrassed ourselves.

$\mathcal{S}$ave the life

of a helpless animal,

and you have done

the work of God.

Forgive yourself first. Only after you have allowed yourself freedom from your own regrets can you let go of grudges toward others.

Admit your weaknesses,
and you are halfway to
conquering them.

✦

A mirror is only as good
as the reflection in it.

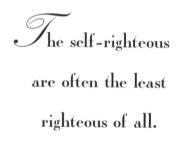

The self-righteous

are often the least

righteous of all.

If everybody

says you're wrong,

you just might want

to reconsider.

If you are lost,

remember—you have merely

taken a detour on the way

to your destination.

$\mathcal{T}$he river of time
flows at its own
unchangeable pace,
even under the bridge
to the Millennium.

The safety net of

friendship will catch

you when you fall.

When we
sympathize with someone,
we know; when we empathize,
we understand.

A two-faced

co-worker is more

treacherous than a

temperamental boss.

A mother nurtures

her child long past

childhood.

✦

*W*ork is only one

part of life.

Beauty feeds the eye

but does not necessarily

nourish the soul.

✦

The stars shine brightest

in the darkest night.

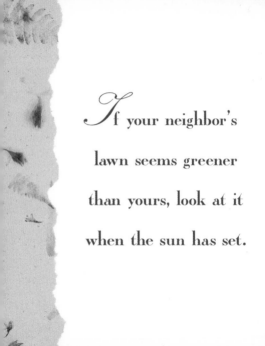

*I*f your neighbor's lawn seems greener than yours, look at it when the sun has set.

I was annoyed when someone bumped into me on the street, until I turned and saw that he was blind.

One warm exchange of words with a pleasant stranger can light up an entire day.

*F*ind something you

truly believe in,

and everything else will

have meaning as well.

In the throes of indecision, a deep, inner voice will whisper an answer.

The sun is a friend to
those who do not mind
getting burned.

✦

The tides of time
wash away even the
deepest despair.

*W*hen a loved one dies,

remember:

you will go on loving him.